Bare Bones

Feel or Be Broken Vol. 1

Chronologically

Lydia Beltran del Rio

Author's Note

It is important to note that these writings are placed in a chronological order. Due to that fact, some of the earlier poems are much darker (and less developed) than some of the later. Though, it is important to note that this book is a journey in grief, loss, heartbreak, and the growth in between. There are some poems here I hope you don't relate to. But if you do, I hope you find some healing in allowing my words to become ours.

— Lydia B.

Bare Bones

Bare Bones

•••≠

Crown

You want to know my feelings?
They're feathered, frayed and torn.
Some days have weeping hours,
While some have laughing grins.
First, I'll tell you of the days I'm down,
Then it ends on a happier note.
Perhaps by then, you'll forget my pain
And think this is all a joke.

You'll see me on those days,
Pretending I'm alright,
Pretending that I'm "*fine*."
Well, I can promise you,
My heart?
Is as hollow as an empty gold mine.
So I'll wear my crown,
My crown of joy.
But wait, yes, hark…
For the thing of crowns is this.
They're too far from your heart,
To touch or leave a mark.

Now I enter the good,
The days I feel alight.
These days are many,
For I tend to live with sight,
Hope and music; or at least so if I fight.
But to most, my mind is strange,
Not many understand its range.
Or why it is so hard to express,
The weight that lives inside my chest.
I'll admit, on "happy days," I wear a mask.
But this mask is for survival.
It hides my pain from myself as well as the world.

Bare Bones

For we all need "good" days as revival.
No heart can take the constant rain.
So fake joy is my lifeline.
I wear it, or I'll drown.

Bare Bones

≠
Fear of fear
Fear of death
Fear of drowning
Fear of breath
Fear of terror

Bare Bones

≠

When is it	-over?
When am I	-done?
Why am I still	-here?
Why can't I	-run?
I just want	-out.
But you make me	-stay.
Right here in this	-misery.
I can't run	-away.

Bare Bones

≠

Nothing

Empty

Full of life

Nothing

Empty

Laugh and smile

Nothing

Empty

Empty

Bare Bones

≠
To slit my wrist
It will never pass
To slit my wrist
And escape at last
My empty thoughts
Need nothing more
Than visuals, to tear and bore.

The feeling gone, it's echo eclipsed
By empty, (empty) and hollow pits
I cannot think
In any sense
Nor pull up words
With meaningness

I stare away at empty wrists
And dream, oh dream
Of all the slits.

While bleeding dry:
When words escape my liquid lips
They shut you out
I make no sense

My words encased
By dripping drops
My heart is spilled
On jagged rocks

Bare Bones

≠
I hurt at nothing
That's what I feel
I stock it up, then peel and peel
The stones away
The wicked thorns
The lucid dreams
The Manic fjords
They flow between my nose and cheek,
And slip deep down,
A cavernous creek

Bare Bones

≠*
My heart feels like fruit getting stuck in a blender.
A juicer is draining my blood and emotion,
And I watch you drink it down.
Giving all my life force to be emptied for you,
I give my precious life force to you.
I drip with vulnerability,

A thing impossibly done…

*

<u>Love Potion</u>
Your love is a potion.
I drink.

Love poison.

*

You are the silver string I wish to line my life with.

•\\≠

<u>On A Grey Day.</u>
These legs aren't mine, but they're mine.
She creeps in, asking for solace,
Feeling wasted, she collapses into me.
"Hold me," she says,
"I need anything you can give me,
I'm barely alive.
I'm trying to stay alive."
A hurt soul radiates.
She can't move any longer.
But I can hold her,
And hug her,
And comfort her broken soul.
Like a little girl,
She's under my wing, and I'm realizing
I'm stronger now.
Not completely, but I'd almost say alive.
I can care for her now.
Where I could not before.

(She is who I once was…)

≠
How long can you hold your breath?
I've been holding mine for years.

Bare Bones

♯*
Your silver Loving heart
Makes me sing,
Sing for only you,
My silver Loving heart…

But the scent of death is mine.

•••≠

Paradise In August
You used to be my home
I know every nook,
And the room other people overlook.
I like it best…
Door wide open and the wind wrapping 'round,
I'd stand.
Arms, wide open.
Heart, wide open.
Eyes of joy, wide open.
But I can't stay,
As I stand at this door, my shoulders slump
And my heart sinks deep,
My breath grows shallow, and here I weep.
I almost jump…
But this fall would not be near enough to death.

You will never be home again.

Never again.

•≠

Lydia's the name, depression is my game.

•≠
<u>Lightning Post</u>
Seems all I'm made of is electric shock.
I'm made to be struck down.

Bare Bones

≠*
End me.
Or should I do it myself?

Seems I'm halfway there half the time.
Half alive,
Half in drive
About to dive…
Off the edge of sanity—
And sanctity—
Is all I can think to hold me back
It cuts the slack
That I dreamed
In the back

Of my mind…

The end.

Bare Bones

♯
Overhead > I'm feeling led to ride the waves of wind.
Undertow < I'm feeling low the strength I held has died.
Overhead > I dream in red, the color of blood and wine.
Undertow < I feel alone, so empty, grim, and tired.

Bare Bones

♯
Death awakes inside my tired, empty mind
And every-thing I held so dear has left my brain behind.

Bare Bones

≠*
So cold and endless is my heart…
Your fist at its door is the only beat left.

Bare Bones

≠*
Empty chambers of an empty heart.
I've moved out,
Maybe you should too.
Before the building comes tumbling down.

≠
Time passes, my joy passes too.
I'm lonely,
Not alone,
More times than a few.

•≠*
<u>Melancholy madness:</u>
Forever I am yours,
And never I am mine.
But why would I choose me,
When I am so blind?

Bare Bones

•;
Tired of the circles,
Tired of the cycles.
What's new to say?
Nothing is changing.
Because our hearts are breaking.
The same and the same.

Yet I reach for you,
And you reach for me.
The same and the same.

Bare Bones

•••*

The strength I earn is gained by tears:
I carry them with me.
Gentle not to let them spill,
I build muscle that no one here will see.

Through the skin of golden embers,
Through fire and light,
I breathe.
Fire that melted your ice-cold heart—
then left me to drown in your sea of sorrows.

Burnt out and broken, I remember…
The drowning.
Before I learned that I *can* dance with the water, that earns
my trust.
Breathe in the darkness you created through us.
That's the beauty I've found,
When you'd rather I'd drowned.
Brought me life in a whole different way.

•^*

You were whispering take-backs that can't be taken back

•≠
I run from my pain.

    And fall on my face,

        Trip over the weight,

            Here in front of me

Bare Bones

•^

I take a breath,

And take a step,

To look around in wonder.

Three leashes here around my neck,

Head pounding much like thunder.

Pain and death and bitterness,

All raging 'round my neck.

The trinity of hurtingness,

All pulling from my breast.

All pulling in my chest,

All pulling me-

deep under.

•

But if I ran less and thought more,
Maybe I would be where I wanted.

Bare Bones

•\\≠*
I thought to let you have my heart,
For only a moment, you smiled.

When you picked each flower from my garden,
I held out their roots for you to grasp as well.
I fell apart of our own accord...

To fit your mold,
I tore myself to mulch.
For not being "enough," I hated myself.
And then you.
Until I realized "enough" was all I had ever been...

Just far too much for you.

Bare Bones

Bare Bones

Bare Bones

•>

Listening to the bone-crushing silence
I am afraid.
Afraid to love and be loved.
Afraid to hate and be hated.
Afraid that fear will change my fate.
To let you near might let you break.
Might make me ache.
Afraid of your words.
To let you say them,
To let me hear them.
Afraid and lonely here.
In bone-crushing silence.

•>
No,
Nothing makes sense.
But perhaps it's not meant to?
Nothing has ever made more sense than this...

And that.

Bare Bones

•≠#
My eyes have held more pain and sorrow than I could re-
count.
Once again, I stand in front of the mirror:

Why do I hold myself in tears?
No one else will.
I can't take another end.
I can't take any more pain.
I can't take another heartbreak.
My life is so broken and tired
My body is damaged and worn.
How can I ask myself to keep moving?
How can I ask myself to take another step?
How could I ever let myself try again?

I should have been empty long ago...

Bare Bones

•>≠

I can't take another end.
But in the end, it doesn't matter.
Because you love me too much,
And you can't see why I should love you.

Let me love you until you do.

• > •
Fear rules only a fool.
Don't let that be your legacy.

I won't let it be mine.

But we haven't seen the sun since it set in Las Vegas

•#>
<u>In This Moment</u>
You are everything I know.
And everything I need to forget.

It would be so strange to be a stranger to you.

> •

I am walking on yellow sand.
Empty pockets in foreign land.
Nothing to claim here but
Young hopes and dreams,
And road for miles.

•

You drove away today.

It's a lot colder here without you.

•>\\
I saw the boy with the blue eyes, and he saw me.

Bare Bones

•••>
Time for me is like a flower.
Life exists in moments,
On petals,
Gently layered one edge over top of another,
Just as memories are in a room.
Some places layered thick.
One million moments,
One million petals.
Some falling gently, forgotten.
Some standing vibrant against the rest.

Where memory is thickest, I find the bud,
The center of it all.
Today that is this room.

My memories,
They hold you close in this room.
This place,
These petals,
Layered so many times over…

•••

And I think that it's those with passion who grow…

But I want more.
I don't want my dreams,
I want a reality that makes me never need to reach for the
pretend.
Because in the end—
What more could a dream be…

Than a better reality?

•••>≠
Fear and My Lover
With loose fingers and a heavy tongue, I tell it to depart.
Find its place somewhere else.
And my heart lets it go.
My lover and my fear.
But in this, the letting go, my fear is different.
I fear that fear will come back…

My fear says *fear* is the lover that always returns.
My fear says *you* are the lover that leaves with a question
mark on your mouth.
With those words, fear takes me by the hand and drags my
face to its own.
Drawing my eyes.
In a way that I can only *hope* to see a face beyond its own,
It whispers,
"Let only the bird fly that you are willing to lose."
And I fall to my knees.
Because I don't know if I can lose you.
But I know I will never jail you with the lips that speak of
love or the heart that opens slowly.

I know the words that fear won't let me place my trust in.
The whispers you spell to me of a dream far away.

(But god, I hope they're true.)

Bare Bones

•>
Can you carry me over the threshold of fear?
Yes. You have.
Can I trust you, you'll hold me?
I'll find out from here.

Bare Bones

•

I'm afraid to be needed,
Afraid to be used.
In the old town, I'm fleeing,
My mother's heart bruised.
Maybe someday I'll fly here
and make it my home.
But today, I am leaving,
And I'm leaving alone.

Bare Bones

•≠#>
We walked here,
But now I'm driving because I can't walk alone.
And I remember how to,

But today I need to be okay with forgetting.

Bare Bones

•>

It's hard to lay here, here on my own, without you.
I struggle to remember not to do nothing with my time

I feel so lonely all alone.
I don't know how to be by myself—
Not by myself.
I'm alone, not
On my own…

Who am I, alone, not on my own?

•>

So many of your "word"'s are momentary made-up things.
I understand.
But you brought,
And broke
Me into it.

Bare Bones

•#>
You don't say what you feel,
And if I was there, I would know.
But you're not here,
And I'm not there,
And that's the point...

Entirely.

Bare Bones

I'm done.

Bare Bones

Bare Bones

Bare Bones

Bare Bones

•≠#>

But aren't you already mine?
How could you say goodbye?
I'm dripping with regrets.
Over things we('ve) never said
The words we('ve) carried for days at a time
The thoughts that ran right through us for the weeks that I
spent crying.

All the heavy lifting.
All the weighing worries.
Never finding order

With all the things we're missing…
All of the moments gone missing

Bare Bones

•>

I can't unknow
What I know,
But I want to.

I can't unknow
What I know,
But I want to.

•#>
For the first time,
Ending doesn't mean hatred.
And my heart doesn't know how to take that.
Doesn't know what that means.
For the first time,
My heart only has sadness to hold it at night.
Thank you.

Truly.

•>
You helped me heal.
Now I choose to grow.
And we'll be fine,
My heart and mind.

My heart and I.

•>
We were right to end,
But I don't know if I like being right this time…

Bare Bones

•>\\
The Matrix and the Vibe: a love story.
Late in the night or early in the day,
So many places we ran away.
Together in our hearts and in our minds hoping one day
They would take our lives far away… from here.
And then we could say:

"Look what I've been, and look what I've done, and I've
done it with you by my side."

#•••
<u>It's a great day</u>
but those feelings that I felt
are trying to be feelings that I feel,
and I'm feeling,
like I can't feel like that anymore.

I have these feelings...
but these feelings that I felt are so distant,
that these feelings that I felt, I stopped feeling.
and the feeling of not feeling these feelings,
feels like joy.

I have a feeling that these feelings—
feeling like forever— never stopped.
and I'm forced to feel feelings
that I never want to feel again.

I felt forever forced
to feel feelings
that felt like a fever.
for days,
for nights,
for years.
and felt,
never for quite forever,
the feelings disappear.
but forgetting these feelings,
feels like unforced drops
of... maybe this is happiness?

•>

There are words I simply cannot share here.

•>

I wish I could be selfish and myself, giving away my un-
known years

To: you.

And I.

And us.

I wish I knew if I was yours to keep

Or if it's time to weep.

Weep, and grieve a life I lost with you.

Bare Bones

•>\\

I want my love to dance on your lips and marry your
thighs,

I want to breathe in the moments we lay time behind and
make love.

Lay out our souls

Preach to each other the meaning of love

In our song without words

That only we can sing…

This was our love within love.

•>\\

I'll make poetry with my thumb on your chest and my head on your heart.

The words will be 'love and 'adventure.'

•>

I will be yours for as long as

I don't know…

Bare Bones

•>\\
I laid out my heart.

You laid out your soul,

And I held you that night.

On my mother's couch,

With tears on your face, and tears in my eyes.

That night a fire burned bright

And I knew a new part of your soul like it was always in my hands.

I love that piece of you.

I love that memory more than most.

I'll hold it close tonight.

On this lonely night.

I don't have to let you go just yet.

I still have a piece of your soul…

In my memories.

Bare Bones

•#>\\
Maybe too many tears slip out.

For the shadow in my bed,

And the phantom in your arms.

I want(ed?) it to be you.

I want(ed?) it to be us.

I was only half afraid of it…

it seems you were terrified.

•#
Why in our blood

Is it easier to hate the one we love

Than to mourn them?

I have never felt so lonely, all alone…

•>
There are angry words I cannot share here

Bare Bones

• >

It's not that you left me,
It's that you left us.
You drove away from what we had with a knot in the veins
that bring regret to your heart.
That bring love.
So that when you reached day five in your destination,
I was nothing but the pastime originally intended.
Not with malice did you woo me.
But with the child inside you fighting to find what he
wants.

He thought for more than a second that it was me.

•>\\

It's been two days since I've recognized a day passing by...
It's been four since the end.

Bare Bones

●●●>

And yes,
I will mourn you.
And yes, it will be dramatic.
And yes, I do, and will hurt.
And yes, I will hope that a part of this hurts you too.

Because I have to bleed the love out of every drop in my
heart.
Let loose every breath of yours I held in my lungs.
Before I can live again.
Without the terrible hope that we will *be.*
The hope that dies in my throat every time
I swallow my pride— my fullness of self—my,
"He will regret the loss of this beautiful heart."

But the longer I hold my tongue to the back of my aching
throat and the tears in the back of my whispering mind...

The more I will break in the end.

Bare Bones

•>\\
The lines of love and hate intertwine.
Tugging, in turn, a war of momentary memories.
This time love is winning over hate:
The faces you make while you play your guitar.

•>
You cannot erase every second my heart beat in your chest.

Bare Bones

(Subtle, intimated, calculated, unpromised promises)

•#>
He made careful promises,
knowing my heart would let him take them back,
of all the places we would see.
The places our hearts would live...
But when he said *"we,"* he meant *"I."*

•>

<u>I was always the indigo sky</u>
For so many years, a storm ripped through my mind.
It found beauty in its own pain.
This year I pulled the rippling thunder clouds back,
And we taught my stars to shine again.

Bare Bones

•>\\
From:
Me

To:
Silence

•>\\
My mini heart breaks
Every time you're not at the top of my stairs.
And I know,
You may never be again.

• > •
Do you?
Even know how lonely you are?

•>
There is rain in my heart.
Holding blood and teardrop memories,
In the heavy breathing veins of my
Heavy heaving heart.

•>
It's 1:18 am.
It's 10:18 pm.

Bare Bones

•••>
But first.
Find the thing that guides you through the maze, that is
yourself.
You will find your way out.
I'm sorry that I could not walk you through,
And I'm sorry.
For the times I tried to drag you through the ramshackle
walls you've built.
The times I wanted to take control
and steer you out of your tunnels.
The ones only you can find your way out of.
The ones you dig your heels and nails into when someone
tries to drag you out.
You will find your way.
Out on your own, I hope you find your way.

I'm sorry.

Bare Bones

•••>\\

Mansion

I met you at the front, and your eyes greeted mine, shim-
mering like the ocean
and there was a curiosity I had not expected.
I stood at arm's length of your cracked open door and found
myself knocking to be let in.
I did not hold fear as I stepped into the foyer of your mind's
mansion.
I'm so glad we danced at the forefront of our minds that
night.
As I met you slowly, as you let me walk through your
beautiful and scarred halls, I saw your story, the lines writ-
ten along each corridor, I saw the rooms where you found
yourself, the ones that love and the ones that hate. I saw
your story through blue eyes and read between the lines
with brown.
When you got lost in your train of thought or found your-
self in a winding staircase, I touched your hand and held
you, tried to guide the way out.

Like this, I learned you faster than you've learned your-
self. (bold, I know)
I have walked willingly with you into rooms full of rage
where your fingers dripped red, rooms full of white where
you let music paint pictures of your life for me...
And rooms that were empty. Where we built our own mem-
ories and found each other in ways, no one ever had before.

Then, and I don't remember how... but I found myself back
at your door.
To the one, I had first entered.
And with all of my knowing, your inside and out,
I could not see what it meant.

Bare Bones

Until I saw your blue eyes only in pictures with blue skies,
and I was forced to realize…
I was being left behind.
And I was outside again…

This time when I reached to knock, I found my fist at my
side.

•>\\
I saw you…
Hidden deep within the cracks and ridges of your heavy-
laden heart
And I loved you.

•••>\\

In your car, when you drove like you had no life to live,
Nothing else you could give…
To the world.
I held nothing but slumbering rage in the depths of my
chest
And a pit of "what will happen?" Slowly shoving out of my
stomach.
How do I let you? And let you?
I hope I did you right that night.

I tried to take your fist and pull you from your head's
confusion.
I wanted to pull your heart through the winding maze
you've built,
And race around each terribly tall wall like a warrior ready
to save you from your own despairing heart… only this
time, I could not see the way back.
I was slow to the draw…
I hope I did you right.

Bare Bones

•••>

Words catch in my mouth,
Float on my fingers,
Twist in my lungs.
I looked again where we used to be
and found nothing in its place,
but maybe a shirt of my own on the ground where you once
played a song.
I saw you living there.
Here in this room, you were here.
Your heart was alive but not set right… where it wanted to
be.
Unfortunately for me.
And for you…
So many places you want to be, but none hold as many ini-
tials as me.
Two. Hearts.
Or two letters…
You know what you chose.
And I don't blame you.
Not because I don't know my worth
but because I know you haven't found yours.
And that's alright. Because you will.

And I hope I was a step along the way.

•>
I wonder in all of my life,
When I will lose this broken heart and find a way without
you.

• •

I let my life become a mess to find something beyond the loneliness

•

With my heart in my hands and the moon at my side,
I run to the feeling of the empty side of my bed.

Bare Bones

>

You think I'm so stuck in my past because you've never met yours.
You keep it an acquaintance in the back of your mind and hope that one day it will disappear into someone you never really knew.
You've met it once or twice in passing but never stayed long to chat.
Thinking you're better off not knowing.
Not getting to know
Your own past.
Your own self.

Bare Bones

•••>

From day one, you chose to name yourself the starving art-
ist.
Rather than a boy without a job, who only half lived for an-
ything.
You named yourself many things.
Rather than facing the truth of a world, you couldn't admit
you were choosing

To live in.

Bare Bones

•>
But you were never in it like I was,
But how could I expect you to be?
But how could you,
Not expect
Yourself
to be?

Bare Bones

•#>

And I guess I'm not 'in love with you.
Because in order to be in love 'with you,
You would have to be in love *with* me.
And I can't be 'in love with you all on my own.
So guess I have never been 'in love with you.
Simply in love—
With you…

~

You find things in your heart that you cannot explain, so you name them God and Satan.

•

When and where did my mind

Find this padlock,

That not even *my own* heart can unlock?

Bare Bones

•>

My heart may long,

It certainly mourns.

But Darling, I am A-Okay without you in my arms.

I know it, dear,

You won't be here.

Certainly not with hands above your head.

You will only appear in these words right here,

And my far too tangled fears.

Bare Bones

•>

I yelled at you, I even swore.

And fought with angry words.

But maybe, dear, if you'd stayed here,

We'd end without a score.

Bare Bones

•••>

I reign in the rain,

It tries to leave my eyes.

But tonight, I know I've cried

Too many tears inside my mind.

My eyes will dry,

And leave the weeping to the leaves on my back porch.

Bare Bones

•>

But I do wish you were here,

To be forever in my arms.

Despite my heavy words

And the fears I try to hide.

I know your heart

I know your mind

I wish I would not have to leave them behind.

But I do.

Because I can't grow me right now.

Because I must grow me right now.

While you are growing you.

Where you are growing you.

•>

<u>2nd Call</u>
Tears in my eyes from the wind

or my sighs.

You wish to be fine.

I wish *we* were fine.

•>

It's hard to breathe in these too tense moments.

But I heard your voice in my ear once again.

Bare Bones

•>
You called again.

I want to know you like I did.

The parts that are harder now…

I want to be there to soften their blow.

But it's not my place, and you've made that clear.

I'll just have to stay and miss you from here.

I don't miss the anger; I don't miss the fights.

I miss the way you squint your eyes.

The twitch in your lip when you look too deeply into my

eyes…

I miss the good times,

Perhaps idolized in my mind…

Idealized.

I miss being free to love you.

Goodnight…

•>

The thing you hate about me is that you can't listen long enough to catch my words.

Or maybe I'm just unable to express myself as well as I think…

•>

I still miss you even when I'm mad.

Even when logic says otherwise.

•^#>

Logic & Daydreams
Logic and Daydreams live in a house,

It is me.

Logic and Daydreams live in a head,

It is mine.

Logic tells Daydreams, "Do not miss the love you lost.
Only heal and forget the pain it caused."

Logic hears Daydreams: "But for Darling, for Dear, my
heart was a mosque. A temple of knowing and loving, un-
paused."

Logic says, "Daydreams, don't forget it was tossed…."

Logic heard Daydreams— "Yes, but Logic, without him,
my future feels lost."

Logic holds Daydreams and pulls her in close. "But our
heart, it will heal… Don't let us be the cost."

•>

I love you.

I know that it's not alright,

But I still love you.

•#>
My heart, no my head.

Needs to drive faster than I ever have before,

And scream out the pain that haunts me.

Bare Bones

•>

I'll try to convince myself to stop loving you.

I'll try to convince myself I'm fine.

I'll let you convince yourself you're over me.

I'll let you convince yourself you're fine.

I'll try to remind myself you cannot be mine.

I'll try to remind myself that I will be fine.

•••≠\\

My White Knuckles
braced for empty impact.

I held my breath like no one knows.

Like I cannot breathe, so I won't.

Like no one needs to know.

(Like maybe you would have if you tried…)

It is no weakness. It is strength.

It is my strength.

The strength I found alone and in my own…

Mind.

In my own fiberglass heart.

Why did you judge my splintered heart?

The one I put back together with my own hands, my own
loving words.

I know the little girl who died that night.

I hold her tight and rock her gently.

I carry her in her slumber and bring a never empty well to
her bedside. I know how she wept and how she held it in.

Maybe she is who I live for.

She is.

She is who I live for.

She is who I smile for.

Bare Bones

She is the girl I dreamed I would not always be.

She is the girl I almost was forever.

She is the girl I will never push away.

She is who I saw in you.

She is who reached for your heart.

"Remember me?"

Is not a question she hopes I answer,

It is a fact.

She will be healed every day from the hard supply I've now come by.

She will never be alone again.

•

I'm growing here like I never have before.

Not in speed but in strength and in stride.

Thank you, Apartment 5, for being who you are to me.

•>\\

Can't you taste the way 'I miss you falls from my tongue?

•>

And in some ways,

I can't believe you've done this.

And in others,

I know I should have seen it coming.

But isn't that sad?..

•>
You owe me more than a walk through my door.

•>\\

These sunshine days give me life to keep breathing.

The moon reminds me what I've lost.

•

I can smile without him.

I just wish I didn't have to…

•>

And even in the moment, I told you what a woman I had become,
I was such a little girl.
Because I will always be a little girl trying to grow older in the things I've never learned.

•

If you didn't think, for just one moment, what thoughts would come to mind?
Vent to me if you're willing:

Bare Bones

•••>

I think I wished that I could dream of forever throughout all
of 'Us.'
But I never let my heart hope for more than a moment.
I knew my heart would break right in half if I pictured you
under the tree
With the falling stars and their gentle glow and have it
never be so…
So I nearly never did.

I never let myself see you there with me.
I never gave much time to our long-lost future.
I see no logical way it could have ended there without a
broken wing and a broken neck, but I wish I could have
wished for it.
Because then there could have been hope
Allowed in my heart.

Bare Bones

•>\\
"Whose car are we taking?"
"You wanna drive?"
His phone,
His wallet,
His keys.
A three-pocket man.

• •

Don't be so afraid to live life a day at a time.
That's all it is.

When your heart needs a break, give it.

Bare Bones

•>•

I'm alone, and I'm lonely, but that's okay.
I'm alone, but that's good.
I miss you, and that's okay.

•>
It will break my heart,
But someday
I will have to move out of this heart for you.

• >

The only words at risk to rip your heart apart,
Are the ones you know speak the truth.

Bare Bones

••• >

<u>Pause</u> >‖
You know why I stayed so stuck in this place?
You put my heart on pause.
In the moment you left my life
I began to grow in reverse.
I had to heal the infected wounds that grew as your finger-
tips uprooted the heart intertwined with mine.
My heart's break exposed and breathing.
Barely…
In the aching…

I had to let my weathered tears rain down their love in my
heavy aching heart.
Fill every pore so tenderly
There's a healing hand I've had to learn to hold
My own.
Until each wound grew slowly,
From their deepest depth,
To the surface.
Scar tissue.
Shallow.
Healing with hesitance.
Hoping, maybe,
you'd come back

But you won't.

(Or at least not for a very long time…)

•>

<u>Beautiful</u>
Holding a mask above your face,

Pulling it tight every moment there might be an ounce of caring.

It's been this way for years.

But this year, I'd dare to say,

That almost changed.

Bare Bones

•>\\

It's odd how

<u>you</u>

are the only ones who truly

left,

And the only one

with the nerve

to tell me not to be upset about it.

Bare Bones

•-

I search for solace in the stars.

The stars, they are my friends.

In the - silent - nights,

In the - siren - nights,

In the - empty - nights,

In the - city - nights.

They wink there gently.

Maybe I lay and lay my thoughts below their gentle gaze.

Maybe they listen intently, reminding me gently,

I know my heart's intent.

It is their never pleasant job to hear the hurting soul's gentle sob.

For the night, in its beauty, brings silence.

Maybe the silence is comfort.

•>

There is so much peace in the near-silence.

There is so much pain in an accidental memory.

•>\\
Lightning rolled in on our dead-end summer.

Bare Bones

•>

You ran far away,
So I ran to my words.

You ran from your fear,
So I ran to my words.

Bare Bones

_____Bean Baby Chronicles

~ __^^

This little devil is more than she appears,
I forgot your shocking sense of adventure.

~ __^^

Keep your beans out of my poetry.

~ __^^

I liked you much more before you bit my hand at
3am.

~ __^^

Because of you, my wrist aches, and my fingers
begin to bleed.
My fists grip whatever shield can cover my
tired body,
My tired eyes.
Because of you, I've lost my sleep.
Because of you, I'll lose my mind

~ __^^

It's too late to lay down arms,
like you never used a sword against me—
Never bit my thumb.

~ __^^

You crawled back into my arms too late,
There is no time left to heal the wounds you gave us.

•>

My empty side seat sends me sidelong glances…

Through the rearview mirror's peripheral vision, I saw:

How very not there you were.

Bare Bones

•

It's not whatever.
It's a song full of angst,
It's a poem full of pain,
It's a day full of crying and heartbreak.

Respect that.

•>
I feel the pain of loss like:
Maybe it was never gone before…

•>
I struggle with anger and
confusion and
love.

Bare Bones

•>

The notes you played on an album.
(They are so in my way.)

Yes, I can be a bad bitch without you.
Get out of my way.

(Please…)

●

Overthinksville.
That's where I live.

Bare Bones

•>

A breath of fresh air and a stab in the heart all at once.

I feel my heart's home,
My heart is home…
And so far from it.

Thrown across the breeze,
It is somewhere along the road to the mountains and the
sea.
I hear its beating slow as it heals
And breaks
In the waves of wind.

Searching to find its place.

Somewhere far from home…

Bare Bones

•>

When I remember to regret letting you go,
I regret to remember...
your heart couldn't let us win this time around.

All the loss is futile.

•••
This time, my smile is not false.
Somehow neither are my tears.
I think that I am learning from life,
That it's not only one or the other.
I can be devastated and not be depressed.
I can be heart-broken and not break.
I can find happiness even when my heart aches,
And things don't go as I'd hoped.
I am both: brokenhearted and happy.
Today that's okay.
Today that is good

Bare Bones

•>

Don't believe the loss never hurt me.
Don't forget I'm hurting from the inside out.
My smiles are not fake, but neither are my cries.
The ones that find their home in the darkness
On a night alone,
When everyone I know
goes home to their lover.
And my heart remembers,
to ache for you.
It cannot forget,
the ache for you.

Don't forget that.
Even when I smile.

•

And maybe I *did* take a detour that is slower than the road ahead.
My mind couldn't take those moments of silent.

(Those seconds of stagnance.)

Madness will catch my mind if my body loses momentum
In this moment.

•>
Roses are red,
I am blue,
Every time I think of you…

I do wish love would choose to prevail as it does in the
movies.

Bare Bones

•>

It's so hard to be both.
In my mind, you are mine.
In my heart, you are mine.
But I must be reminded.
You are neither.

(I wonder what it means when I sleep on your side of the bed?)

•>
<u>Stranger</u>
to the one I love
I wonder where you are, who you are?
We lost a lot that day.
Isn't this exactly who we never wanted to be?

Strangers…

•>

<u>Like a phantom limb</u>

I've cut you off, but here you haunt me still.

•>\\

There was a falling in deeper than ever before

As I held you in the moonlight, in the back seat of your car

•>

It's 2:15 pm

It's 11:15 am

Bare Bones

•••>

I couldn't understand, but I think I tried.

I know I tried.

But what a child I was a month ago.

What a child I was three months ago.

Two days ago.

Today.

I am twenty years old.

Twenty years older than I was three months ago.

I am twenty years old.

I am not such a child anymore.

I am not eighteen, so young and naive.

I am twenty.

I am still young, still naive.

Never knowing what I will know in three months.

Only knowing I know more.

Only wishing today

That I was not so old with my little experience.

That I was not so young with my heavy experience.

With my little knowledge.

Bare Bones

With my young mind.

Too young and too old.

Too far gone,

Not far enough.

I've learned all I know from heartbreak.

Bare Bones

•>

Maybe you ran from fear you could not overcome

To a fear you could prove had no hold over you.

An impressive mind, an impressive move.

Bare Bones

•••

<u>Today,</u>

One of my best days, I've lain alone in never quite silence,

Listening to the words of other lovers.

Other lovers of the words art and poetry.

Other lovers of the world of art and poetry.

Other lovers.

So steady is my breathing brain stretching gently, or not so,

In a pose so unnaturally natural to its tangled limbs.

To my tangled limbs that could not stretch today for more than five minutes.

For more than five minutes.

Because today is my brains day.

The place I love to call home and hate to come home to.

The place I love to build on, stretch, expand, add an addition,

Build onto the house I call home.

Where my heart loses its mind and lives only in quiet to allow the thoughts my head knows all the while,

to breathe in their sighs,

and let loose their everyday tension.

Their every day tension.

Their tension.

Their everyday tension.

Bare Bones

My mind needs attention from not just my soul but my mind.

Do not silence it. Don't say, "not now."

The heart can mourn for days for nights, but today is the day for my mind.

Give it the stage.

Not the back of your mind.

Give it the stage.

Not the back of my mind.

Give it the stage.

Bare Bones

Written for the girl inside my heart who could not put this pen to paper:

•••≠\\

Once Upon a Lover:

There was a love for depression I held in my hands.

I grasped tightly the locket meant to hang around my neck.

The locket?

The pendulum?

The thousand-pound weight in a pond exactly 5foot 2inches deep?

A swamp?

A heart's demolished childhood and its desperate search for anything in darkness?

Perhaps if I was not in love with its understanding of my soul, I would not have given it my heart's open casket.

When my lips could not move, my heart sang:

"Bury me deep, oh beloved depression.

Bury my sorrows in so many blades of grass that no fire can ever reach the soul.

Help me forget that they lay awake in my bed beside me.

Help me snuff them out so they can never breathe again."

This is why I choose to drown.

Bare Bones

In hopes that with my heart, the pain stops too.

The deep confusion that: never will my heart find a way.

Its never-ending alleys buried only one quarter of an inch below the surface.

It is enough.

There was a way only she could hold me close...

The way she lays her laced lips in the back of your mind and digs her nails in deep with the gentle grasp of:
"I've got you when no one else - does."

"I've got you when no one else - knows."

"I've got you when no one else - understands."

There is a comfort in the deep melancholy of:

"Fuck this, I don't care to mask my face."

"Fuck this, I can't."

She holds me like a cloud in darkness.

Like lightning and thunder in the night, she caresses my soul.

Patting my back with her comforting hands,

With her fisted hands.

She grazes her beautiful nails across my back,

Her razor nails.

In a way of distorted comfort...

Bare Bones

In her way of disastrous comfort.

But who else could touch the darkness in my chest?

So she lays at my bedside, ever caring,

ever ripping my heart apart.

She was with me when I could not breathe.

When I held my breath for fear of life.

She was with me when I laughed with death in my eyes.

When I knew not who she was.

Don't you understand?

I am afraid of the one that I love

Her name is life

Her name is depression

Bare Bones

I remember that despair, though I have grown beyond its hold.

It yanked my heart out in the moments after death.

Truly,

Had I had access to another dimension in the moments that I grew too old before my own eyes, I would have taken it gladly.

In my own way, I did,

And she was it.

She once was my lover.

Bare Bones

•••

Though I have to wonder:

What truly happens when one stops breathing?

I hope to never know.

But I will one day

Or I won't

Or it won't matter

But aren't those things the same?

Bare Bones

•••≠\\
<u>It Begins With an 'H'</u>
I know too much of a building I don't want to understand.

Why does it feel like a comfort, like a haunting comfort, to remember its halls?

Why was the young girl who walked there so challenging herself in a race to remember?

It was all too much of a game to me.

Something I couldn't understand.

I feel like, 'what if I went back? (As if I could.)

To the little girl who stepped only in the circles on the carpeted hall.

Even when it meant looking young and wild and stupid.

Even when she had to bend backward to reach her only hope of distraction.

She could not understand. It was a game.

It was a temporary upset in the life she had hardly begun to lead.

It was nothing. Inconsequential.

Now it has shaped my life.

How horrendous of a turnout it was for her, but who am I today?

What part of myself am I not proud to be living in?

What parts would I change? Truly I cannot know in whole.

Besides, my jealous nature, and my naivety…

Bare Bones

But when will I not be? Naive and a child?

The day that comes is the day I fear as much as the day is long.

That is to say— it depends on the day entirely…

I hope most days to be content in the day that it is.

For that is all I have, one day at a time.

Carried only by moments.

I have had so many by now, but not nearly enough.

Never nearly enough, only far too many.

Sometimes far too many.

Far too many,

And never enough.

Bare Bones

•••\\>

I miss the times that happened here,
So carelessly, each day passed.
I wished them away until the moment I could be with you.
But by default, I must have wished each day away en-
tirely…
How odd to not notice the moments you long for until they
are gone… over.
I hope you're happy.
I hope you truly are living a happier life.
I hope right now, at 8:34 pm on August 4th, 2020
you are writing alongside me so far from me.
Perhaps about me?
Right now, at 5:34 pm on August 4th, 2020.
I hope so.
But I can only hope…
Play music, my love.
Make music.
I know your heart needs it.
I hope one day to hear it.

Bare Bones

~

The smallest sparrow flies alone.
Overhead it lays its wings to the air in a push so heavy it
knows it will not fall.
I wish I had that assurance in my own self.
There is no fear in its height.
No fear in its landing.
What a wonderful thing to be a sparrow.

.

Bare Bones

•>
You live so ingrained in my mind,
I forget not to imagine you must miss me too.

•>
So you did it!
You broke your word
And broke my trust.
I hope it did for you what you wanted.
Because it certainly did nothing for me.

Bare Bones

•&>

The love for a family I should not love.

I miss the mother and even the father.

I miss the brothers and even the girlfriend I hardly spoke to.

Not only do I miss you, I miss your grandmother

And the way it felt to walk into your parents' home.

Your cat-dog and your too-dark basement.

The front room where you first held me close.

And the sliding door at Christmas.

It does not compute.

How could it be gone,

So quickly?

●

There is simply too much for a six-week session
Or a 'fix-my-depression.'
Then leave.

Bare Bones

•>
There is a slideshow in my mind.
A way I see the way you stood.
In ten thousand seconds all at once.

There was:
A moment, a second. You leaned against the wall playing
me love songs.
A moment, a second. You wrote songs on my bed, and
broke at the core for the words erupting from your heart.
A moment, a second. You danced with me in my mirror the
day you drove away.

Bare Bones

••• >

<u>I am afraid</u>
to remember too much of my love for you.

It has not disappeared.

Only, like a mirror or ring, tarnished in time.

So that maybe I can't see quite so clearly who we were and why I should be sad to see it grow muddled in my mind...

You were so many things to me.

So many wonderful things that I cannot count them.

Or name them.

Or ever fully forget.

Because, in truth, there are so many pieces of the person you are that I will be unable to find myself without.

In any love or friendship.

I am afraid of these words that I've laid in my hands.

I run away to another place to escape their embrace,

but I know there's no hope of forgetting...

Because you.

Are in my mind these days.

You hold my heart in your hands even still while I try,

(like my body on an early morning of work, but you're holding me so close I cannot want for anything but to stay,) to force my heart to roll away,

to escape the hands, it can only be held in.

How was nine months, not four years.

Or more?

How was nine months, not four years.
Or more?

•••

Oh, but wouldn't it be easier to believe in a love that

never leaves

Bare Bones

•\\>

The day you left, I cried and wept.
And watched you drive away without a second glance—
And I don't know how I held my breath…

As unsteady as it was.

•>

My heart likes to keep forgetting that you left of your own
accord.
That you knew the outcome and let me go before I even
had the chance to say, "please go, I'll be fine!"

Bare Bones

•>

There is a love for you I held in my hands.
Gently you told me to close my fist around it,
and put it to rest in the pocket of my jeans.

Bare Bones

•>

It hurts so much to say…
You weren't the one.
Not who you were to me.
It was simple in my head
but never in the way I had to fight for you or your clarity.
This you is not the one.
I wanted you to be…
It's so sad, so horribly sad that you aren't…
I love you nonetheless. But I can't let myself hold on to you
Or our love
Any longer.
It hurts.
But I hope for my heart's sake this is the beginning of truly
getting not just past but over you…
I loved you…
I loved you.
I loved you so much that in so many moments, I couldn't
put a name to it.
In so many moments, you were so much to me, it could not
be given the name love…
And as I stared out the window, out the view we always
shared, it broke me again and again thinking,
'I don't think I can do this letting go.'
My body quakes in sadness, and forgiveness, and regret.
But I have to accept
We were not right to be one and the same.
On this night, as I lay in my bed
Awake for lack of your presence.
I have to let you go…
And forgive us both for losing a love I held dearer than my
lungs in a time we meant to grow
Together

Bare Bones

Love is not meant to hurt.
Love is not supposed to hurt.
Love is not meant to leave.
Love is meant to build.
Love is meant to grow
Together

_____
If you are happy in love,
Healthy in love,
Hold on to love for the rest of us.

•>
We talked…

You did most of it
You looked at me like your love never died
I made a joke about you begging on your knees…
You said, "don't stop writing,"
I said, "you can't stop me…

I wish that was your homecoming, not your apology for
leaving how you did…

Bare Bones

•••#>
Keeping his heart behind a door
Just out of my reach…
Lock it tight.
But wait, the door is open on the other end of the hall.
Chase it… there he is, who he truly is.
But the moment you reach out to catch his arm, he's gone.
Door locked. No sign of entry or exit, just… gone.
Maybe up the staircase?
Maybe down the winding corridor?
In the garden?
Maybe around every corner and behind every wall.
So nearly in reach as to hurt you slowly.
Wear you down…

Bare Bones

•≠
<u>My roommate, my depression.</u>
My roommate leaves me lonely,
she leaves my room a mess.
I turn my back on cleanliness
Then find it in a wreck.
I live a day in peacefulness,
then find she's torn it up.
My roommate is my closest friend
She likes to call me 'stuck.'

Bare Bones

•••#>

I feel like I'm losing you and losing time to be with you.
But you're probably fine, and that's not only odd,
but terrifying.
It's been hard again since August, since July…
I'm running because I'd like to be fine.
I want to be fine.
I'm desperate to be fine…

But I'm not.
Because seeing you triggered every good memory that
hangs between us.
Limp.
Limp from our forgetfulness…
I want to run from my fears.
Every moment I live inside my mind
I realize the waste,
I see the skies,
I see the change
Around me.
There is no time to waste…

Limp… from our forgetfulness,
Limp from the jolt in my step
every time I try to move away from you.
Every time I try to move toward you.
I am spinning as an unending clock chimes 12

Am, Pm, Am, Pm, Am, Pm, Am, Pm

Time cannot stop, and neither can my wasting it as I spin
on the spot
and wait for the end of this hole I am digging.

Bare Bones

I was done writing about you.
I was almost done writing about you.
I was going to stop writing about you.

Why are you here in the back of my mind—
In the front of my head.
In the wishes I drink,
and the air that I breathe (too quickly), as I think of you.
Why are you here to haunt my days and devour my nights?
My memories carry me as a phantom to your nearly bed-
side…
As near as sanity allows,
The park down the road,
the coffee shop two blocks away…
where you might find me one day.

Might.

Probably won't…

Won't.

But why waste time wasting time?
Why waste years when I want them with you.
Because you don't want to waste them with me.
But how can it be a waste if we both want it?…
So then you must not?
But you do.
I saw it in your eyes,
But your voice said goodbye,
(Said otherwise,)
And I'm so unafraid of the things in my brain that I've put
them here in writing…

Bare Bones

•••&...
The love of a father so often forgotten to be missed.
Life has almost always been without...
Without my father.
Perhaps I forget that I've not needed one...
Or that I simply learned to live without.
When I see the face of a father forgotten by his children or
the face of a father who lives so naturally in his role, per-
haps I forget that I don't need one at all.
That I've learned to live without.
Manuel.
A father I did love.
A father I must have lost if I had one...
I believe only sometimes that I did...
In both senses.
I forget the loss that has come to me too heavily, too young.

•>
Fuck you.
I'll try my best not to

Bare Bones

•>
Can we meet in the day?
Can we talk in the day?
Because daytime is the only
time
I can trust myself to speak with you
And not *be*
with you.
Because the nighttime was our time.
Our time to be lovers.
The daytime was our time,
Our time to be friends.
Best friends
And lovers
That was the beauty and magic in us.
In our time.
Ourtime.

Bare Bones

•>
I think there must be a line
Where our day turns to night
Where our days turn to nights
And our eyes meet in a line to our lips
Then align at our hips
And we crack our composure

Bare Bones

•#>
I have to build boundaries with you.

Because you can't have my body without having my heart.
You can't love my body without loving my heart.
Do you want all of me?
It's a lot to handle.
But you can only have both.
Never one or the other.
Only both.

Or so I'd like to tell myself

to tell you…

•••&...
I lost my father when I was young.
14 perhaps?
Or 12... or 21 by the end of it.
I can't forget or pinpoint the age that I felt.
In the moment, or in the moments, it haunted me.
I can't remember, but I couldn't forget, even when I was convinced
I had...

Forgotten.

Was there never a moment I could have been truly numb?
I know it felt like nothing but death...
But wasn't that the point?
It felt.

Like death?
To me...
I guess I wouldn't want my father to flip through the pages of my books and memories.
Not the ones that speak of loving too much on a broken heart,
Or the ones of death wishes.
Surely not the ones on losing everything I believed...
I wonder if it would even upset him?
Even break his heart?
Or if he'd forgive himself for never putting real meaning to the words, he would pray for my mother's sake... was it only for hers? I wonder?
Or was it for his as well?
Was he grasping at straws as he was being grasped at by death?
Or was he truly believing in the end?
I hope if he did, it was true.

Boys, don't get me suicidal
They wish they had the chance.

•••
I know fear will never leave.
But I hope to dull my fear of fear.

Bare Bones

●●●>

I wonder if I wander the wrong way in these times.
In the moments I look into your eyes.
I think not, I think I keep my head straight.
Or I think so
Until the days
I spend alone in my room without you,
And I realize my mind has done nothing but lay and wait
and distract from the seconds that stretch like hours, in
minutes—into hours.
And the day is done without having begun
Because I paused in wait for something, I cannot have…

Bare Bones

•••&...
I ran to the beach to visit my dad.
Not because he's here but because my memories are.
And tonight I need advice.

I keep missing calls from an old friend.
I keep forgetting to remind myself to write.
The minute I come home, I just lay alone; I say I'll nap at
the end of my shift, but I just lay there on my phone.
The symptoms of depression, but I don't know how to fix it
this time, and I know that this issue isn't temporary.

I'm going to the beach to visit my dad.
He doesn't live here… only my memories do now,
But tonight, I need advice.

Bare Bones

•••
I should have known,
by the way, you moved in alone,
you would not have let me in had the mountains shifted
west,
or east, as the case may be.
You have decided to do this on your own
And in your own
Time
Making daily the dose of not laying open
And daily, the dose of not caring much.
You cry alone and on your own
Time
In your own mind, you release the fear and never let it
cross
mine.
Never let it cross into the open world around.

Only short-tempered friendships,
And maybe they don't mean much to you…
Don't put in too much effort!
Or you might have to fear the feeling of being me.

•>

I would be half of who I am without you.
Not because you complete me,
But because you encouraged me to complete myself.

Thank you.

•>

My Pillows are meant to be you

•>

<u>I nearly love to fall apart</u>

I know the pain so well…

But I do love to fall together again.

The ache of the break, feeling healing in the moments my breath catches the tears on my lips, and your hand on my cheek when I find once again

That we cannot take the distance between our hearts or our bodies.

I love to fall back into you.

I will only break completely when I know it will never happen again.

Bare Bones

•••

I have a love for poetry and how it makes me feel.

It helps me breathe and escape and release and embrace and decide how I think out loud in the safe-ty...

Of my own forgetful mind.

In a way, I can retrace my steps and relive the beauty of understanding a soul.

Maybe it's mine

I forget...

but I love it.

Bare Bones

•••\\>

You dropped off my key on the day my life fell into place far away from you.

Not so far that I can't feel the ache.

I'm going away without you.

I'm moving away without you, and I still can't believe you'd let go of me like this... like you have...

I know this one took your strength.

In a time, we meant to grow apart,

How we fell back together...

•#>

How were you in it for the worst moments...

And not in it for the rest?

•#
How did the day come so quickly that I pack away my memories

In boxes that don't fit them.

Bare Bones

•

My cupboards are empty, so are my walls, my clothes have no home.

I'm driving away from the memories of us, not for the last time.

But for the first of too few

The intimacy we held between our eyes,

In our fights and our making up.

The way you held me in your car when our hearts might be breaking will never fade to nothing in my mind.

I loved you for that.

I fell in love with you with that greatly in mind.

I was so sure we could talk through anything in our way,

In the front seat of your car.

Bare Bones

•••

My last night here…
I love it dear-ly.
This place
Where my memories lie thick like the closing bud of a rose.
This couch, I'm giving up. Where we sat so many days and laughed so many nights…
You wrote music here, I wrote poetry.
It's too bad this ugly couch can't live on through the ages with me.
It truly is hideous, though. And takes up too much space.

I can't pass these last hours slowly (enough)
All I can do is lay to rest my body in the plush comfort of my home one last night.
Goodnight, Apartment 5, you've served me so well. I won't forget you.

Thank you.

Bare Bones

Bare Bones

•+

Fifteen minutes away, that's where I've always been.

And when you break or fall, I'm there until the end.

I love you more than any friend

Though you'll never be my lover.

You've always been my greatest friend

I'll never need another.

Bare Bones

•#\\>
Did you even tell me one thing?

One thing that helped you fall to loving me...

If you did, I don't remember.

I saw your eyes, I heard your voice, I felt your heart and lit-
tle actions...

But did you even tell me one thing?

Bare Bones

•#>

I didn't stop to say goodbye, and I regret it now, and deeply.

Not because I can't stand to be away,

Nor to remember the way your arms wrap around me, which,

god, I have forgotten…

But because I went back on that promise to myself.

The one where I said, "fuck the world and their broken stone walls.

I will feel what I feel and live it."

But I held back that day, two days ago.

And I passed through your town weeping out the confusion that's soaked into my bones like sponges just waiting to be pressed…

There is still so much left.

Bare Bones

Bare Bones

Bare Bones

Bare Bones

Acknowledgment

Many people have carried me and this book through the last two and a half years of writing and editing. I could not have done it without them. First and foremost, I would like to thank my very best friend Kelsie. Because of her, this book and I are here today. She is the person who has listened to my every disjointed thought from the first poem to the last, and beyond. My brain would breach if I had tried to write and live through these moments without her. Thank you to my sister Abby, for reminding me who I am every step of the way, and somehow knowing exactly how to balance on the line between honesty and kindness in order to encourage my growth. Thank you so much to Ivey, my dear friend who has not only graced us with her illustration and cover art, but has helped me to start building this collection from my notes app during a very lonely 2020 summer. "Thank you" is not enough for my favorite teacher and strong supporter Mrs.C, (if you know her, I'm sure she's inspired you too!). She knew I would be a published writer before I did, and made sure to tell me so. Thank you to my Mom, Laurie, for her patience, comfort, and listening ear, as well as significant help in proofreading and editing as one of the first readers of my manuscript. The adorable teddy bear is thanks to Corey, an unsuspecting artist and kindhearted friend. Thank you to my dear friend Lydia S. For helping me see life and heartache from a new point of view, always encouraging healing, and teaching me the importance of boundaries. Thank you to Mikkel for being the friend I did not know I needed and giving me the safe space and cold water to grow. Thank you unendingly to Tim and Danielle, as well as the ranch staff and team, who helped healing become an option for me after my first great loss. Last but never least, thank you to each person who has read my art and found a connection, no matter how small!

Bare Bones

About the Author

Lydia Beltran del Rio grew up on the coast of west Michigan and currently lives in Chicago, Illinois. She has used poetry as a form of personal healing for the greater part of her life. Bare Bones is her first published piece.

Made in the USA
Monee, IL
06 February 2023

27202288R00125